I0409524

Thrifty Traveler
Building Wealth While Exploring the World

Table of Contents

Chapter 1. Introduction

Dazzling landscapes, bustling city streets, serene mountain trails; isn't this the world you yearn to explore? But does it seem like your bank account is holding you back? Well, we have wonderful news for you! Our Special Report: "Thrifty Traveler: Building Wealth While Exploring the World" gently merges the magic of sightseeing with practicable financial wisdom! This illuminating guide is your passport to gain financial stability without compromising your wanderlust, striking a fascinating balance between breathtaking adventures and savvy money habits. Bursting with cost-cutting strategies, dynamic wealth-building tips, and a gazillion ways to enjoy every corner of our beautiful planet, this report will fill your heart with joy and pockets with savings. Here's an invitation to immerse yourself in this project and embark on a journey of a lifetime, all the while building your financial future. With this Special Report, traveling on a budget will no longer be a dilemma, it'll be a delightful adventure you'd want to buy into!

Chapter 2. Introduction to Thrifty Traveling: The New Age of Adventure

In this dawn of globalization, when every inch of the planet seems at our fingertips, too many people find their desires to see the world stifled by financial constraints. But we're here to tell you that being a traveler doesn't necessarily require deep pockets. It calls for a spirit of discovery, a curious heart, and only a modicum of economic nous. Behind the dreamy Instagram posts of exotic locations lie the underappreciated realities of budgeting, saving, and smart spending. And it is in this sphere that we offer you the much-needed counseling.

2.1. The Myth of Expensive Travel

Travel, as we know it, has been marketed as an expensive endeavor meant for those with ample disposable income. Media and our perception have equated travel with luxurious beaches, five-star hotels, and premium airlines. However, this couldn't be farther from the truth.

While such comforts are beautiful experiences no doubt, they don't define travel. Travel is about exploring the unknown, connecting with diverse cultures, savouring local cuisine, and discovering yourself amidst the alleys of history and lanes of nature. Essentially, travel is an enriching personal experience that stretches way beyond the materialistic confines of luxury.

A closer look at the travel stories of numerous globetrotters reveals the extraordinary experiences they had with humble budgets. Remember, a snapshot of an adventurer in a conical hat paddling through Vietnam's Mekong Delta can hold far more character than a staged photo-op in an infinity pool.

2.2. Welcome To The New Age Of Traveling

The advent of technology has revolutionized the way we travel. The luxury of research, that earlier generations of travelers didn't possess, has bestowed novel opportunities on us. We now have at our disposal things like comparison websites for tickets and accommodation, real-time traveler reviews, digital maps, and guides, e-books, travel forums to seek advice, and many more.

What's more exciting is the rise of budget-travel culture. More and more young people are seeking adventures over comfort, experiences over opulence. Immersion in local culture, house-sharing platforms, and cheap street food are suddenly as enticing (if not more) as packaged tours, opulent hotels, and multi-course meals at high-end restaurants.

Moreover, the pandemic-induced shift in work culture has led to the possibility of long-term travel while working remotely, and subsequently, an even more cost-effective way of seeing the world. This is going to play a pivotal role in shaping our travel decisions in the post-pandemic world.

2.3. Thrifty Travel: Your Route To Financial Freedom

While the very phrase 'budget travel' may sound a bit daunting initially, you will soon appreciate its offerings. It is not about penny-pinching in unfamiliar territory, rather it's about making smart decisions that help you sustain your explorations longer and save money for future adventures.

Think of it as a lifestyle change rather than a temporary fix. It involves developing habits like saving more, spending less, and investing wisely. It might even entail picking up new skills that could be used during travel, such as learning to cook a few basic meals or understanding the basics of auto maintenance.

Budget traveling does not mean you must compromise on experiences, it means prioritizing what matters the most - the essence of travel itself.

2.4. Becoming A Thrifty Traveler: An Exciting Adventure Ahead

Your journey begins, not when you take that flight to an exotic location but when you take the first step towards understanding the dynamics of financial wisdom and integrate it with your wanderlust.

In the following chapters, we'll share actionable strategies for cutting costs without cutting corners, investing your money wisely, and looking at your finances with a long-term view. We will focus on creating a sustainable model that would not just save money but also help you build wealth over time.

Remember, the beauty of travel is not the destination, but the journey. We invite you to embark on this new adventure, this new way of thrifty traveling. Because we believe that the road to financial stability should not be a barrier to the roadway you want to traverse.

We promise that you'll come out of it not just as an avid traveler, but as a savvy individual aware of the ins and outs of financial independence. Because in the end, isn't that what travel is all about? Gaining new perspectives, understanding the world, and emerging from the journey as a more enriched and aware version of oneself. Your adventure awaits. And, as they say, the first step to an incredible journey begins here, today. Happy travels and even happier saving!

Chapter 3. Setting Financial Goals: Your Travel Roadmap

A journey of a thousand miles begins with a single step, and your journey towards financially savvy travel begins with setting clear, defined goals. Financial goals will serve as your North Star, guiding your money-saving efforts and illuminating your path forward.

3.1. Why Set Financial Goals?

Having a clear objective can give purpose to your savings and make the process of budgeting not only easier but also significantly more rewarding. Without a specific end in sight, it's easy to feel lost and overwhelmed. Financial goals, then, are your roadmap, your GPS, showing you the shortest and most manageable route to your desired destination.

But don't mistake a financial goal for a magic wand that instantly aligns your finance. Think of it more as a compass, guiding you in the right direction.

3.2. Understanding Your Financial Goals

Everyone's financial goals will be different, depending on their personal circumstances, long-term plans, and of course, travel dreams. Perhaps you plan to backpack across South East Asia or to relax on a cruise around the Mediterranean, ride a bicycle across Europe or explore the wild mysteries of the African savannah. Every journey has a different budget, and thus a different goal. So let's start by understanding what type of financial goal you need to set for your trip.

There are three kinds of financial goals - short-term, mid-term, and long-term.

Short-Term Goals: Any financial goal you aim to achieve within a year comes under this category. For travelers, this might include saving for a spontaneous road trip or an inexpensive vacation.

Mid-Term Goals: If you aim to achieve your financial goal between one to five years, it falls under mid-term goals. This could be covering the cost of a more extended vacation, such as a cross-continent backpacking trip.

Long-Term Goals: Any financial goal that you seek to achieve in five years or more is a long-term goal. For travel enthusiasts, this might mean saving up for that once-in-a-lifetime luxury round-the-world cruise.

Energy spent now in identifying which category your travel plans fit into will be energy saved later in avoiding aimless and frustrating saving efforts.

3.3. Get Specific

Once you have a broad idea of your travel goal, it's time to get specific. Break down your financial goal into practical, manageable steps. This could mean figuring out how much you need to save each month, what financial sacrifices you might have to make (like skipping that daily latte), and how long it will take you to reach your goal.

It's also crucial to account for the costs you may not consider at first glance. This includes not just the cost of flights and accommodations, but also spending money, travel insurance, visas, vaccines, gear, and an emergency fund.

3.4. Charting Your Course

Now that you have determined the kind of goal you are working towards and fleshed it out with specifics, it's time to plot your course.

Start by establishing a monthly or weekly saving target. Knowing what you need to set aside each cycle can make the goal feel more attainable. It also takes the guesswork out of budgeting because you'll have clear numbers to strive toward.

Keep track of your progress. Visualising your progress can keep motivation high, and give a real sense of achievement as you tick off smaller goals on the way to your larger target. There are many free apps and templates available to track your progress, or you can go old-school with a simple pen-and-paper chart.

3.5. Reaching Your Destination: Your Savings Plan

Finally, figure out how you will save the money to meet your goals.

There are several savings strategies you might choose to employ. For short-term goals, this might involve cutting discretionary spending or taking on extra work. For mid-term goals, it could involve investing in a high-yield savings account or mutual funds. For long-term goals, tooling your retirement account or buying property might be the way to go.

Remember, it's not the size of the step that matters, but the direction. Financial goals, like travel, are a journey. Go easy on yourself, be consistent, and watch as you slowly but surely turn your travel dreams into reality.

3.6. Adjusting Your Sails

Remember to revisit your financial goals frequently. The economy fluctuates, personal circumstances change, priorities shift, and sometimes, the journey itself changes you. Make sure your financial goals are keeping up.

Using your financial goals as a roadmap for your travel dreams can make saving less stressful and more rewarding. After all, every dollar saved is a step closer to your next adventure. And with a clear roadmap, you can start ticking off destinations and achieving your travel goals, one journey at a time.

Chapter 4. Budgeting Basics: How to Finance Your Wanderlust

Imagine a world where financial constraints are not the first hurdle to your dreams of adventure. Imagine being able to book that trip to your dream destination without the lingering fear of financial ruin. It sounds idyllic, doesn't it? But we assure you, it's not only attainable, it's fully within your grasp. This crash course in budgeting basics will help you lay the financial groundwork for your dreams of exploration and adventure.

4.1. Set a Goal

First thing's first, before setting off on your odyssey, you must determine your financial goals. Are you aiming to traverse the country on a tight budget or do you have sights of an extravagant trip? Feel free to dream big but ensure that your goals are concrete, achievable, and tailored to your financial capabilities.

4.2. Assess Your Income and Expenses

Now, onto the nitty-gritty. You need to gain a comprehensive understanding of your current financial situation. Pile together your receipts, bank statements, credit card bills, and salary/wage slips. Compare your income with your expenses, and evaluate the areas where you can save.

Of course, life would be easier if we all had a surplus of cash right from the start, but most of us need to find ways to generate savings.

Make a habit of tracking your expenses, identifying necessary costs and areas where you can cut back to grow your travel fund.

4.3. Create a Savings Plan

Creating a savings plan will introduce discipline and clarity to your financial plans. Your savings plan will serve as the roadmap to your travel aspirations. Commence with determining the amount you need for your travel. Then, calculate how much you need to save each month to reach that goal.

Make your savings plan realistic and flexible. Understand that there will be months when unforeseen expenses occur; adapt your plans to cater to these changes, so you always keep moving forward.

4.4. Control Your Spending

One of the most critical aspects of budgeting is learning to control your spending. Start with creating a daily, weekly or monthly spending limit based on your projected savings goals.

4.5. Make Money Work for You

It's not just about saving; it's also about growing your wealth. Invest your savings in low-risk instruments like savings bonds or high-interest savings accounts to let your money work for you.

4.6. Be Debt Smart

If you need to use credit to fund your travels, be smart about it. Look for credit cards with travel benefits or rewards, and always have a plan to repay the debt as soon as possible. The goal here is to avoid unnecessary interest payments that can drain your travel fund.

4.7. Emergency Funds: Your Financial Safety Net

While maintaining a staunch focus on your travel fund, it's crucial to remember that not all savings should be intended for travel. Allocate a certain portion towards an Emergency Fund. This safety net will protect you from unforeseen circumstances without hindering your travel plans.

4.8. Cutting Corners without Cutting the Fun

Traveling doesn't always have to be expensive. Search for budget accommodation, cheap flights during off-season, and free attractions. These cost-saving alternatives will help you stretch your budget and enable you to experience more.

4.9. The Art of Negotiation

When traveling, mastering the art of negotiation and bargaining can save you significant amounts of money. From markets to transport arrangements, don't be afraid to haggle and seek a better price.

4.10. Dine Local

One of the quickest ways to burn through your travel budget is dining in touristy places. Venture into local eateries for authentic and cheaper dining options.

In conclusion, budgeting is about making the right choices rather than limiting yourself. This journey towards financial freedom is daunting, rewarding, and full of self-discovery. Embrace it, adapt as needed, and remember - the world awaits you, not just for you to see, but also for you to master the fine balance of wealth and wanderlust. As you turn these tips into habits, remember that every financial decision you make is a step towards making your travel dreams a reality.

Chapter 5. Mastering the Art of Frugal Yet Fantastic Traveling

There's an unspoken perception that traveling always leads to skyrocketing costs. Whether it's transportation, food, lodging, attraction fees, and miscellaneous expenses, the costs stack up and might seem daunting. However, with the right approach, traveling doesn't have to burn a hole in your pocket. It's all about understanding the art of frugal yet fantastic traveling and implementing some simple, time-tested strategies.

5.1. The Power of Planning

A little forethought can go a long way in making your travel plans surprisingly affordable. Thorough planning involves more than just picking a destination and deciding the travel dates. It should encompass all elements of your vacation, from transportation modes to meals.

1. **Destination Decisions:** Thoroughly researching your destination before you arrive helps avoid unexpected expenses and overpriced tourist traps. Check the currency rates, local customs, and average costs for accommodation and food in the area. That way, you're prepared and can create a reasonable spending plan. Remember, not all destinations are created equal, and choosing places where your money stretches farther can result in significant savings.

2. **Expense Estimation:** Draft a rough estimate of the trip's cost based on your research. Include not only the obvious expenses like airfare and accommodation but also meals, attractions, souvenirs, and any potential unexpected costs. A well-thought-out

estimate can guide your daily spendings and prevent you from exceeding your budget.

3. **Itinerary Creation:** Detailed itinerary prepares you for potential expenses while ensuring you see and do everything you want. Plus, you can take advantage of discounts and deals if you buy tickets or make reservations in advance.

5.2. Affordable Transport Hacks

Transportation is often one of the largest travel expenses, yet it provides the greatest opportunity to save money if approached efficiently. Here are tips to trim down transport costs:

1. **Smart Flight Bookings:** Understand how airlines price their flights. Prices fluctuate based on day of the week, time of year, and how far in advance the flight is booked. Use flight aggregator websites and apps to compare prices and dates to bag the best deal.

2. **Land Transport:** Once at your destination, choose public transportation over taxis or rental cars. Not only is it a fraction of the cost, but it's also a great way to immerse yourself in the local culture.

3. **Shared Ride Services:** Also consider shared ride services or bike rentals in cities where these services are available. They're often cheaper and more environmentally friendly.

5.3. Where To Stay Without Breaking Your Wallet

Accommodation can consume a huge chunk of your budget, but there are ways to reduce this expenditure significantly.

1. **Homestays and Hostels:** Consider staying in homestays, hostels,

or budget hotels, all of which are less expensive than traditional hotels. These alternatives also offer a more local experience.

2. **Book in Advance:** The early bird catches the worm – and the best rates. Booking your stay in advance can lead to considerable savings. Many establishments ramp up their rates as rooms begin to fill.

3. **Consider Location:** It might be cost-effective to stay a bit far from city centers and major attractions, where rates are typically higher. Be sure to weigh the cost of transport to those attractions from your outlying location - sometimes it is cheaper overall to stay close to the places you intend to visit.

5.4. Savvy Food Savings

Saved on transport and accommodation? Great! Now let's tackle another significant expense – food.

1. **Local Markets:** Buying from local supermarkets and cooking your meals can save you a bundle. It's a fun and unique experience, as you get to try local produce and learn to cook local recipes.

2. **Street Food:** Street food is an affordable option for meals on the go. It's also a perfect way to get a taste of the local cuisine.

3. **Water Bottle:** Carry a refillable water bottle. It's environmentally friendly and saves you from buying expensive bottled water every time you're thirsty.

5.5. Free and Thrifty Sightseeing

One of the joys of traveling is visiting attractions and making unforgettable memories while exploring. Here's how you can do it on a shoestring budget.

1. **Free Attractions:** Many cities around the world have popular attractions that are free to visitors — such as museums, parks, walking tours, or historical sites. Always be on the lookout for these places.

2. **Tourist Passes:** For cities with paid attractions, consider purchasing a tourist pass. These passes offer entry into multiple attractions for a single fee and can be significantly cheaper.

3. **Hiking:** Outdoor adventures like hiking are usually free, and they provide an invaluable experience of exploring the natural beauty of your destination.

Mastering the art of frugal yet fantastic traveling is all about balance. With good planning, smart choices, a little flexibility, and a keen eye for deals, you can go on the magical journey you've dreamt of, without fearing the drain on your finances. Live your wanderlust, explore the world, and keep your financial situation healthy and thriving. Travel should not be about extravagance but experiencing new cultures, sights, and experiences. And with the above tips, that experience won't cost an arm and a leg.

Chapter 6. Practical Hacks: Save Big on Accommodations

It's an all-too-common story: a perfect vacation budget derailed by whopping accommodation expenses. Not anymore! Let's embark on a journey to unearth valuable insights and practical tips for saving big on accommodations.

6.1. Consider Alternative Accommodation

In the era of modern travel, hotels no longer hold a monopoly. Unique, eclectic, and often more affordable alternatives await explorers willing to veer off the traditional path.

Hostels, often seen as the province of young or solo travelers, can make a fantastic budget-friendly choice. They frequently offer single beds in dormitory-style rooms, shared bathrooms, and communal kitchens. If privacy concerns you, don't fret! Many hostels also provide private rooms at cheaper rates than hotels.

Holiday rentals are gaining popularity too. With platforms such as Airbnb, Homestay, or VRBO, you can rent a variety of properties worldwide. From comfortable studios in city centers to unique lofts in the countryside, these platforms offer accommodations to suit every taste and budget.

House-sitting or home exchanges offer another route. Websites like TrustedHousesitters, Housecarers, or HomeExchange serve as platforms where travelers can stay for free at someone's home while the owner is away.

6.2. Timing is Everything

Understanding the art of booking can save you a small fortune. Most accommodations have dynamic pricing, which means the price changes based on demand and time.

Try to avoid peak travel periods. The cost of accommodations can skyrocket during school holidays or local festivals. Booking during the shoulder season (the period just before or after the high season) may yield better prices and fewer crowds.

Always keep an eye out for special deals or packages. Many hotels offer off-season discounts or bundled packages that include meals and activities. Platforms like Expedia or Booking.com often have limited-time offers. Set up price alerts and be prepared to snatch up deals when they arise.

6.3. Don't Shy Away from Haggling

While it might not be standard practice in some parts of the world, in others, bargaining over the price of a room is standard procedure. Don't be afraid to negotiate! Be respectful, smile, and you might just secure a great deal.

6.4. Go Directly To The Source

Don't underestimate the power of booking directly. Accommodations often set aside their best rooms for people who book directly. Not only can this mean a better room but direct bookers often get better service. If there are issues, you might find it easier dealing directly with the provider rather than with a third-party booking agency.

And remember, loyalty pays! Joining accommodation loyalty programs (like Marriott Bonvoy or Hilton Honors) reaps benefits over time. You can earn points for each stay that can be redeemed for free nights or upgrades.

6.5. Consider Longer Stays

Staying in one place longer can significantly cut costs. Many accommodations offer discounts for longer stays. You can live like a local, get to know the area, and save money!

6.6. Do Your Research

Don't just rely on popular booking sites. Do a little digging on local tourist board websites and travel forums. You might find undiscovered gems that offer great rates.

Use online tools and apps like Kayak, Google Hotel Finder, or Trivago to compare prices. Check reviews on TripAdvisor, but remember to read between the lines; sometimes a bad review is more about the person writing it than the place itself.

With smart planning and an open mind, you can transform your accommodation spending from wallet-draining to wallet-friendly without sacrificing comfort or experience. Remember, the world is your oyster, and with these tips, it just became much more affordable!

Chapter 7. Eat Well on a Budget: Cheap Yet Authentic Food Experiences

One of the most enduring pleasures of travel is savouring the local cuisine, a veritable window to the culture and heritage of your destination. However, embarking on a culinary journey while maintaining a budget can be a head-scratcher for many. Luckily, our guide is here to help, packed with strategies on how to indulge your taste buds without causing a dent in your wallet.

7.1. Shopping at Local Markets

Perhaps the best way to control your food budget without sacrificing the authenticity of your meals is to shop at local markets. Not only do you get to engage with the culture and buy the freshest produce, but you also save a significant amount of money.

Look for markets that locals primarily use. There, you'll find a dazzling array of fresh fruits, vegetables, products, and local delicacies. It's a good idea to carry a small phrasebook or translation app, just in case the vendors don't speak your language. Buying and preparing your food - even if it's as simple as a fresh salad or sandwich - can be a rewarding experience in itself.

For those residing in accommodations with kitchens, it's an opportunity to test out local recipes. While this may be a little time-consuming compared to dining out, the joy of cooking and the money saved definitely make it worth your while.

7.2. The Magic of Street Food

Street food is a part of the cultural fabric of many countries, rich in both flavor and authenticity. It's also usually affordable, particularly in Asian or Latin American countries. Sampling these local delights allows you to understand the culinary culture of the region and keep your budget on track.

However, food hygiene is a critical consideration, especially in countries with lower health standards. Look for vendors with high turnover, and always ensure that your food is cooked thoroughly. If you see locals queued up somewhere, that's generally a good sign!

7.3. Embracing Local Meal Times and Customs

Along your travels, remember to adapt to the local meal times and customs. In countries like Spain, for instance, tapas (small plates) are often served free with a drink during certain times of the day. In Italy, you might find affordable pre-set menus during "aperitivo" hours – usually early evening.

By understanding and aligning yourself with the local dining culture, you have a unique chance to enjoy authentic culinary experiences without overspending. Learning about local customs can be as simple as asking your accommodation host or using Internet-based sources.

7.4. Lunch Specials and Fixed-Price Menus

In many places around the world, restaurants offer special lunch deals a.k.a 'menu del dia'. These are typically less expensive than the evening options and often include a starter, main course, dessert, and sometimes even a drink.

Eating your biggest meal at lunch can be a tasty and cost-effective strategy. The same logic applies to fixed-price, or prix fixe, menus wherein multi-course meals are available at a set cost.

7.5. Stay Hydrated

The importance of staying hydrated while traveling cannot be overstated. However, continually buying bottled water can add up. If the tap water is safe, consider using a refillable water bottle. For places where the tap water isn't drinkable, consider investing in a bottle with a built-in filter.

7.6. The Charm of Local Cafes

Every place has its charming local cafes. Apart from your regular infusion of caffeine, these cafes often serve bakery items, sandwiches, and local specialties at a reasonable price.

Whether you're having a breakfast croissant at a terrace café in Paris or sipping chai in an Indian chaikhana (teahouse), these establishments provide delightful yet budget-friendly culinary experiences.

7.7. Cooking Classes

Another exciting way to enjoy authentic local food on a budget is by attending cooking classes. Such classes are a fantastic way to learn about the cuisine, ingredients, and cooking techniques of the region.

The cost of the class often includes ingredients and your meal afterward. Plus, you get the added benefit of preparing these dishes even after you return home, keeping the spirit of your travel alive.

7.8. Self-Catering and Accommodation Choices

Renting an apartment, hostel, or any accommodation with cooking facilities provides ample opportunity for self-catering. Buying fresh ingredients from markets and preparing meals can be economical. Plus, it's another chance to experiment with local flavours.

Traveling and eating well on a budget doesn't mean you have to compromise on delicious and authentic food experiences. With a bit of planning, savvy strategies, and an open mind, you can even enhance your culinary journey while saving money. Our guide aims to empower you to make financially sound and mouthwatering food choices, adding flavor not just to your meals but also your travel stories.

Chapter 8. Local Transportation: Getting Around without Breaking the Bank

In the thrilling journey of world exploration, one of the most critical aspects to consider is local transportation. It's easy to overspend on this aspect without careful planning. This detailed guide will walk you through how you can get around in your chosen destination without breaking the bank.

8.1. Understand your Options

Every destination has a multitude of transportation options, from buses, trains, trams, and metros to taxis, rideshare services, and even bicycles or scooters. Research the options available in your upcoming destination. Some cities have efficient public transportation that will take you anywhere you need to go, often for much less than a taxi or rental car. Others, unfortunately, may not offer such hefty resources, and you may have to rely on various forms of transport.

1. Train/Tram/Metro
2. Bus
3. Taxis
4. Rideshare services
5. Rental cars
6. Bicycles, scooters, or walking

Understanding your options will allow you to make informed decisions about your transport needs.

8.2. Public Transportation: Your Friend for Local Exploration

Public transportation can be your ticket to exploring like a local while saving significantly. Immersing yourself in the local way of commuting can give you a taste of the true culture, besides being cost-effective. Not all cities have comprehensive public transportation systems, but for those that do, this can be a boon.

Trains, trams, and metros often have regular routes that cover major sightseeing spots, shopping districts, and cultural landmarks. Schedules are generally reliable and are available online or in local transit apps. Take the time to familiarize yourself with the routes, stops, and fares ahead of time.

Buses are another cost-effective means of transport. Even in cities where train networks aren't extensive, buses usually cover a broader area.

Local metros, trains, and buses often have discount passes available for multi-day or unlimited travel. Tourist cards are another option that, besides giving unlimited public transport access for a period, can also offer discounts or free entry at local attractions.

Remember, when using any type of public transportation, abide by local etiquette and always keep an eye on your belongings.

8.3. Taxi and Rideshare Services: Convenient but Costly

Taxis and rideshare services like Uber or Lyft are convenient for quicker or direct transportation to your destination. These services, however, are pricier than public transit. They are best used sparingly or when you're short on time, or public transportation is not readily available.

Always make sure to use licensed services, watch the meter, and know the general direction you need to go to avoid being taken on a longer route. Using a rideshare app can help mitigate these issues since fares and routes are settled in advance.

8.4. Car Rentals: Think Before You Rent

While renting a car can offer freedom and flexibility, it can often be an expensive choice. Depending on where you're traveling, there might be nuances like local traffic laws, hefty parking fees, and different driving conditions.

If it's necessary to rent a car, look for the best deal online ahead of time. Often, it's cheaper to rent the car for a week than for individual days, even if you don't use the car every day.

Also, check your existing car insurance or credit card insurance to see if it covers rentals, so you don't have to pay for extra coverage. Always return the car with a full tank of gas to avoid paying the rental agency's higher gas rates.

8.5. Sustainable Travel: Cycle, Walk or Scoot

In many cities around the world, cycling or walking can be one of the best ways not only to save money but also to see the sights. Many tourist-friendly cities have bike rental schemes. Some areas even have e-scooter or e-bike rentals. These are often very cost-effective and provide a fun way to get around.

For short distances or when exploring city centers, nothing beats walking. It's free, environmentally friendly, and you get to see details you might miss in faster modes of transit.

Local transportation constitutes a significant portion of travel costs, but with these strategies, you can manage your finances without compromising your exploration. Armed with this knowledge, you can make the smart choice in local transportation in any destination, ensuring that your journey is both cost-effective and enriching.

Chapter 9. Unearth Free and Affordable Attractions across the Globe

Traveling the world does not have to be an extravagant affair as the world is full of free or budget-friendly activities just waiting to be discovered.

9.1. Unraveling Europe

Let's start with Europe, a continent steeped in history, oozing charm, character, and culture.

1. **The Louvre, Paris**: Go on a Friday or Saturday night from 6 pm onwards, and you can experience one of the world's greatest museums with a significant discount. If you are under 26, it's completely free every Friday, regardless of nationality. Not to mention the first Sunday of every month is free for everyone!

2. **Free Walking Tours**: Many European cities offer 'pay-what-you-want' guided walking tours. Remember to tip at the end, but it's an affordable way to see the city, learn about its history, show local support, and meet fellow travelers. It's a win-win!

3. **British Museum, London**: Among the world-class museums in London, the British Museum is completely free. Its comprehensive collection spans over two million years of human history.

9.2. Discovering the Americas

Shifting our backpacks towards the Americas, there is a potpourri of experiences ready to be enjoyed without costing a fortune.

1. **Free Festivals, USA**: There are countless free festivals happening year-round in the USA from New Orleans' famous Mardi Gras to 'Shakespeare in the Park' in New York City.

2. **National Parks, Canada**: On Canada Day (July 1), entry to all national parks in Canada is free. Canada's national parks are not only stunning but promise adventure with hiking, horseback riding, and canoeing opportunities.

3. **Beaches, Brazil**: Brazil's beaches offer a fantastic opportunity for budget travel. The famous Copacabana Beach and Ipanema Beach are free to access, and nothing beats a wallet-friendly day soaking up the sun on some of the world's most renowned beaches.

9.3. Embracing Asia and Australia

As we journey East, Asia and Australia also offer many unique attractions that won't break the bank.

1. **Temples, Cambodia**: By purchasing a multi-day pass, you can explore the Angkor Wat Temple, and many of the surrounding temples at a modest price. This world heritage site is an experience of a lifetime, and you can break down your visit across several days for the best value.

2. **Food Markets, Thailand**: Food is an essential part of the travel experience, and in Thailand, this need not be expensive. Street food and local markets provide full meals at meager costs.

3. **National Parks, Australia**: Many of Australia's National Parks are free to explore, offering enormous value for money. The world's oldest rainforest, Daintree, in Queensland, is one of them. Walk amongst its ancient, vibrant ecosystem without tapping into your wallet.

9.4. Exploring Africa

African safaris might not be cheap, but there are plenty of more affordable ways to experience this wonderous continent.

1. **Cape of Good Hope, South Africa**: Enjoy this spectacular piece of nature without spending a dime. Take a picnic along and watch as the Indian Ocean and Atlantic Ocean meet.

2. **Hiking Kilimanjaro, Tanzania**: Granted, this is not entirely free, but considering it's the highest mountain in Africa, the cost is relatively low. This journey offers unbelievable value where you are rewarded with breathtaking views and great personal accomplishment.

9.5. Venturing into the Middle-East

The mystery and allure of the Middle-East make it a budget traveler's haven, especially with these low-cost, high-quality experiences.

1. **Floating on the Dead Sea, Israel/Jordan**: This unforgettable experience is at zero cost, except for transport to get there.

2. **Exploring Souks, Oman**: Wander around Oman's traditional markets, known as 'souks', and immerse yourself in the Middle-East's vibrant culture and color, all for free!

In every corner of the globe, there are opportunities to be discovered that prioritize experience over expenditure. With mindful planning and a vigilant eye for budget-friendly opportunities, the thrifty traveler in you can find joy and adventure in virtually any destination. You just need to know where to look! By being flexible, and considering off-peak times and locations, you can save heaps while taking in the wonders of the world. You hold the key to making your own unique travel experiences, full of rich memories and without the rich price tag.

Chapter 10. Investing in Experiences: Understanding the Real Value of Travel

The traditional mindset has often painted a binary portrait of personal finance where, to gain wealth, one must abandon the joy of exploring and experiencing the world. This chapter aims to shatter that perception and show you how investing in experiences, specifically travel, can be smart and fulfilling, with long-term, tangible benefits.

10.1. Building Wealth through Memories, Not Possessions

The world's cultures and most influential thinkers have all agreed on one thing: life is not measured by the collection of material goods, but by the wealth of experiences that shape us and the memories we create. Material possessions, while necessary, depreciate over time, both in value and in the pleasure they inevitably bring.

On the other hand, experiences, in this case travel, promote continuous growth. Travel opens up new horizons, introduces you to different cultures, and helps you realize the universality of human emotions. Every penny put towards a journey curates a gallery of priceless memories that resemble asset investment. This reminds us that restricted spending on material goods can pave the way for regular investments in experiential wealth, built bit by bit with every venture.

10.2. The Power of Prioritizing Travel

The key to becoming a thrifty traveler lies in setting our priorities to align with our passion for exploration, while ensuring our financial stability.

1. Prioritizing experiences over goods: Reducing non-essential spending on material possessions frees up a portion of your budget, which can be better allocated towards traveling and exploring. Start by making a list of expenses that can be cut or minimized, such as dining out, expensive purchases, or unnecessary subscriptions.

2. Creating a travel budget: Part of your monthly savings should contribute to your 'travel fund.' A separate account for this purpose can ensure that you are consciously saving for your travels.

3. Incorporating travel into your lifestyle: Being a temporary tourist might offer you new experiences, but choosing to immerse yourself in the local lifestyle of your destination will more deeply enrich your understanding of the world. It also significantly reduces travel expenses.

10.3. Utilizing Travel as a Means for Continued Education

Traveling is not an expenditure; it is an investment in one's personal development. Traveling teaches you what traditional education doesn't. It exposes you to the realities of life and imparts valuable lessons of resilience, empathy, and adaptivity.

Visiting historical sites, for instance, instigates an appreciation for human culture and heritage. Likewise, hiking through trails or camping in nature creates a deeper understanding of the environment. By actively seeking these varied experiences, you will be investing in nurturing an enriched perspective towards life, culture, and the environment.

10.4. Investing in Personal Networks through Travel

Travel is also an investment in social capital. Meeting new people, forming connections, and learning from them can have profound impacts both personally and professionally.

Interacting with locals could teach you novel ways of looking at life or making sense of it. Such interactions can also serve as networking opportunities that may open doors you never imagined. These social investments may take time to show a return, but they're usually more valuable than any monetary returns.

10.5. Retaining Value from Travel

The benefits of travel last far beyond the duration of the trip itself. Remember, this value is not just what travel brings to you, but also what it imparts to those around you. Sharing your travel experiences can uplift and inspire friends, family, or even your professional network. This can positively impact your personal relationships, work dynamics, and overall societal standing.

10.6. Traveling Smart to Maximize Returns

To make every dollar count:

1. Off-peak travels: Traveling during non-peak seasons and

weekdays will save you a significant amount in airfare and accommodation costs.

2. Affordable destinations: Look for destinations with a lower cost of living. This will reduce expenses for food, accommodation, and experiences.

3. Long-term travel: Prolonged stays at destinations can significantly decrease per-day costs, especially as you can lease affordable accommodations.

4. Keeping a travel journal: Write about your experiences, learnings, and memories. This can later serve as a tool for self-reflection, act as content for blogging, or even materialize into a memoir.

What this chapter strives to convey is that travel, when approached through a lens of financial wisdom, can become a powerful part of your wealth-building strategy. You invest in experiences, personal growth, education, and relationships. The return on investment may not be immediate and quantifiable like traditional investments. However, in the long run, you'll find that, in gaining wealth from your travels, you are becoming a richer, more enlightened individual.

Chapter 11. From Thrifty Traveler to Wealth Builder: Toward a Prosperous Future

From an avid backpacker tracing the trails of Machu Picchu to an urban explorer wandering the crowded streets of Tokyo, every roving spirit often encounters a similar predicament—a desire to meander without burning a hole in the pocket. The ultimate balancing act of financial stability and global exploration can indeed be tricky. However, at the intersection of thriftiness and wanderlust, rests a promising pathway leading to prosperity. Together, let's tread on this enriching journey of transforming oneself from a thrifty traveler into a canny wealth builder.

11.1. Embracing Frugality and Flexibility

The first step to becoming a savvy wealth builder, while continuing your exploration of the globe is to make friends with frugality. Get hands-on with budgeting skills and opportunistic planning. The resolution is simple—practicing relaxed flexibility with uncompromised vigilance. This may mean opting for off-peak travel, considering less-touristy destinations, or even relishing street-side cuisine over five-star gourmet experiences. Remember, every cent saved today is a dollar earned for your future adventures.

Travel when others don't, it's often cheaper, and the experience could be remarkably more authentic. Familiarize yourself with the concept of shoulder seasons—those sweet spots between peak and off-peak times. In this period, airlines, hotels, and tourist attractions often lower their prices. It's also less crowded.

Moreover, be flexible with your flying options. Consider alternative airports, embrace layovers, or be open to red-eye flights. Utilize flight aggregator websites to find the best deals and subscribe to a few to receive alerts about price drops.

11.2. Nurturing a Fiscally Responsible Mindset

A quintessential virtue of a wealth builder is being financially accountable. It's critical to tracking every expenditure, assessing its necessity, and pondering upon value optimization. Every monetary outlay during travel—be it staying facilities, transit modes, meals, or sightseeing, presents an opportunity of mindful spending.

Use apps to help you document and control your spending. An at-a-glance view of your spending patterns can help eliminate waste and identify areas for potential savings. Remember, every dollar saved is an investment towards your next big adventure.

11.3. Embracing Affordable Yet Comfortable Accommodations

Lodging options are aplenty, each with different comfort levels and costs. Choosing a hostel over a hotel not only cuts down on your costs but also opens up a world of opportunities to forge relations with fellow travelers. Home rentals or house swapping options can provide a more homely feel while you explore new territories, while work exchanges or volunteer programs can not only reduce the accommodation cost to nil but also offer a more immersive and rewarding experience.

11.4. Planning Ahead

Planning ahead not only eradicates last-minute anxiety but ensures you avoid overspending due to urgency. Watch out for early-bird deals or plan well in advance for the best fare and rates.

11.5. Canny Money Management

Being frugal does not imply being miserly and missing out on experiences. It's about being smart with your finances. Look out for complimentary services or packages that club multiple experiences at a lesser rate. A wealth builder is always on the lookout for the best value proposition rather than just the lowest price.

Maximize your credit card benefits. Accumulate and utilize flyer miles, cash back, and travel insurance offerings. Remember, every cash perk or freebie saved propels you faster towards financial wellbeing.

11.6. Building Wealth Through Small Investments

The saved money doesn't just have to finance your next trip—it could also be the seed for your future financial prosperity. Start investing in small amounts regularly into reliable, growth-oriented avenues like mutual funds, stocks, or bonds. Remember, the journey towards wealth is progressive - every small step leads to bigger wins.

11.7. Striking Balance

Finally, understand that it's a marathon, not a sprint. Building wealth while feeding your wanderlust is a gradual process. Keep the balance—enjoy the present but secure the future. A seasoned wealth builder is a strategic thinker who knows when to splurge on experiences and when to save for future goals.

In conclusion, transforming from a thrifty traveler to a shrewd wealth builder requires discipline, planning, and a bit of sacrifice. It involves keeping a vigilant eye on your spending, maximizing savings opportunities, and effectively reinvesting those savings for future growth. Embark on this journey with a positive mindset, and remember—every cent saved or invested wisely today will guarantee a financially stable and adventuresome tomorrow.

www.ingramcontent.com/pod-product-compliance
Lightning Source LLC
Chambersburg PA
CBHW072220290526
45794CB00007B/2823